THE
BOOK
OF
ANSWERS™

CAROL BOLT

hachette
BOOKS

NEW YORK   BOSTON

To my mother and father, Doris Anderson and Robert Gillis Bolt.
I am forever grateful for you and your love.

————————

Copyright ©2001, 2018 by Carol Bolt

Cover design by Kapo Ng

Cover copyright © 2018 by Hachette Book Group, Inc.

Hachette Books
Hachette Book Group
1290 Avenue of the Americas, New York, NY 10104
hachettebooks.com
twitter.com/hachettebooks

Originally published in hardcover by Hyperion October 1999

Updated edition: October 2018

Hachette Books is a division of Hachette Book Group, Inc.
The Hachette Books name and logo are trademarks of Hachette Book Group, Inc.

The publisher is not responsible for websites (or their content) that are not owned by the publisher.

The Hachette Speakers Bureau provides a wide range of authors for speaking events.
To find out more, go to www.hachettespeakersbureau.com or call (866) 376-6591.

Print book interior design by KimShala Wilson.

Library of Congress Control Number: 2018935480

ISBNs: 978-0-31644-991-5 (updated hardcover edition); 978-0-31644-990-8 (electronic book)

Printed in the United States of America

LSC-C

10 9 8 7 6 5 4 3 2 1

HOW TO USE *The Book of Answers*™

1. Hold the **closed** book in your hand, on your lap, or on a table.

2. Take 10 or 15 seconds to **concentrate** on your question. Questions should be phrased **closed-end**, e.g., "Is the job I'm applying for the right one?" or "Should I travel this weekend?"

3. While visualizing or speaking your question (one question at a time), place **one hand** palm-down on the book's front cover and **stroke the edge** of the pages, back to front.

4. When you **sense** the time is right, **open** the book, and there will be your answer.

5. **Repeat** the process for as many questions as you have.

GOT QUESTIONS? THIS BOOK HAS THE ANSWERS.

Carol Bolt is a professional artist living in Seattle.

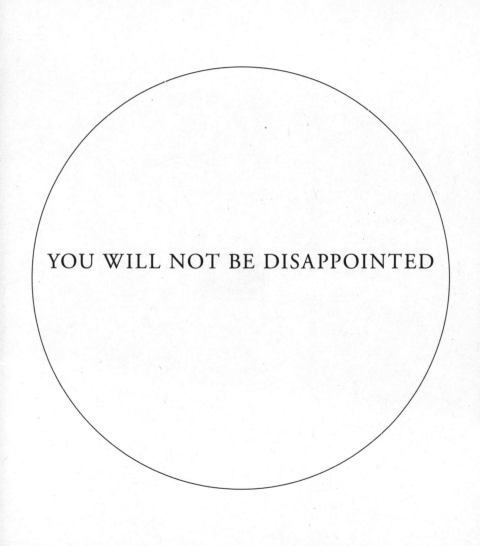

YOU WILL NOT BE DISAPPOINTED

SHOW YOUR APPRECIATION

YOUR ACTIONS WILL
IMPROVE THINGS

DON'T BET ON IT

ADOPT AN ADVENTUROUS
ATTITUDE

FOLLOW THE ADVICE OF EXPERTS

YOU COULD FIND YOURSELF
UNABLE TO COMPROMISE

FOCUS ON YOUR HOME LIFE

INVESTIGATE AND THEN ENJOY IT

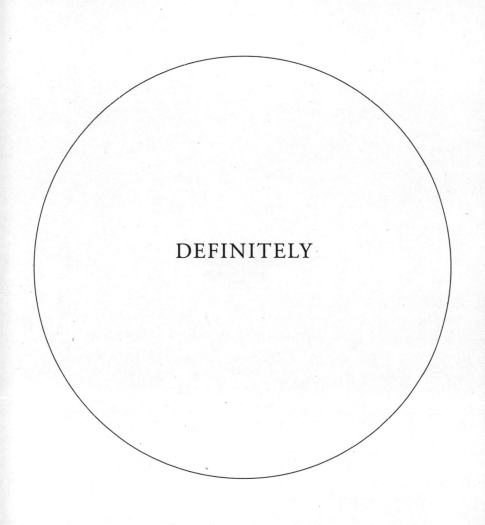

DEFINITELY

ONLY DO IT ONCE

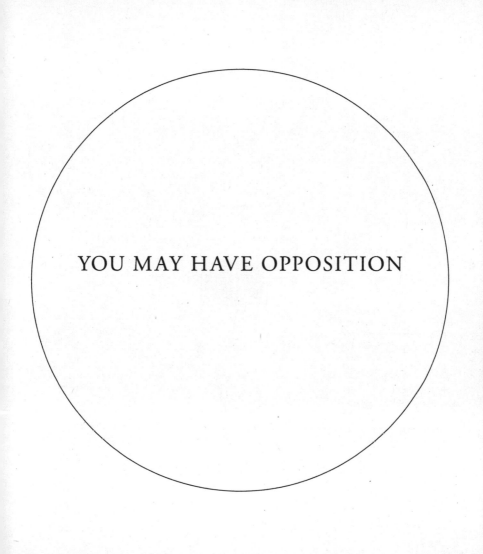

YOU MAY HAVE OPPOSITION

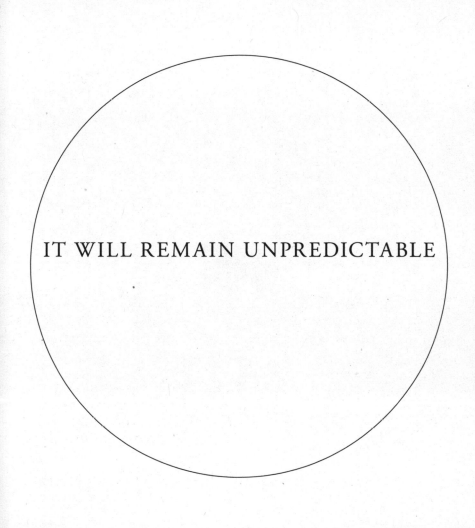

IT WILL REMAIN UNPREDICTABLE

YOU'LL NEED TO TAKE THE
INITIATIVE

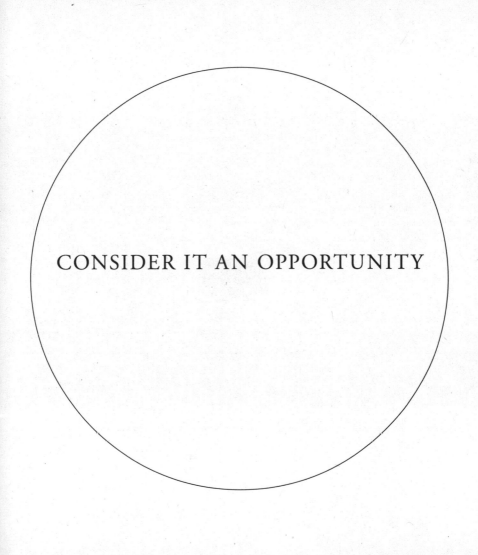

CONSIDER IT AN OPPORTUNITY

BE DELIBERATE

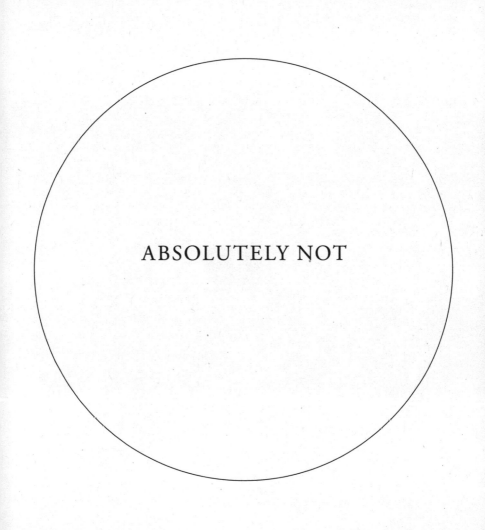

ABSOLUTELY NOT

EXPLORE IT WITH PLAYFUL
CURIOSITY

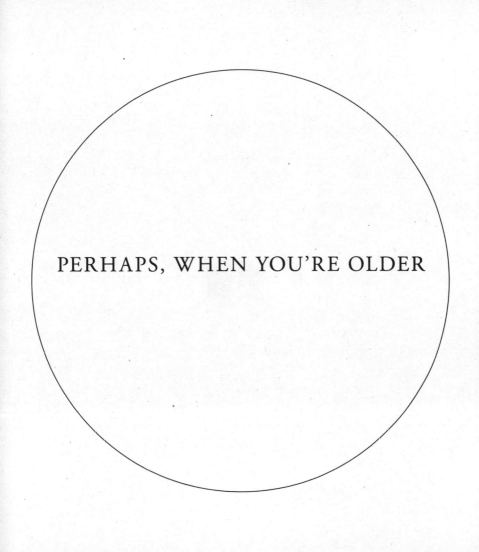

PERHAPS, WHEN YOU'RE OLDER

BE DELIGHTFULLY SURE OF IT

BETTER TO WAIT

REPRIORITIZE
WHAT IS IMPORTANT

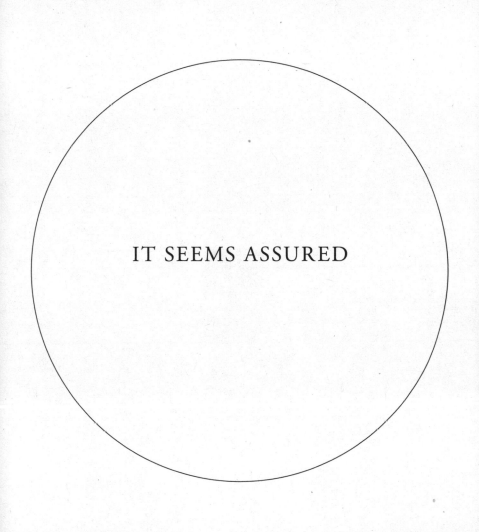

IT SEEMS ASSURED

CREATE MORE SPACE FOR IT

DO IT EARLY

KEEP IT TO YOURSELF

ALLOW YOURSELF TO REST FIRST

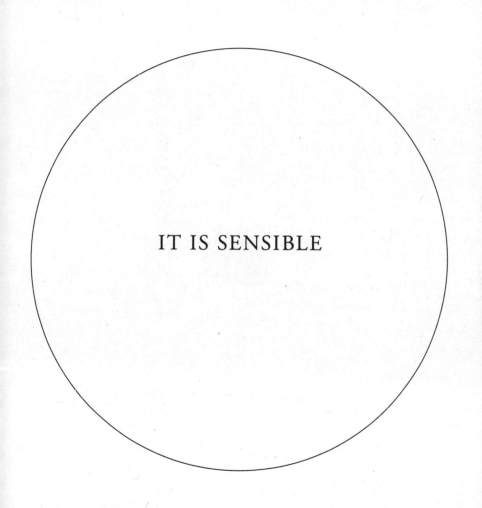

IT IS SENSIBLE

YOU'LL HAVE TO MAKE IT UP
AS YOU GO

STARTLING EVENTS MAY OCCUR

AS A RESULT

THE ANSWER MAY COME TO YOU
IN ANOTHER LANGUAGE

YOU WILL NEED TO
ACCOMMODATE

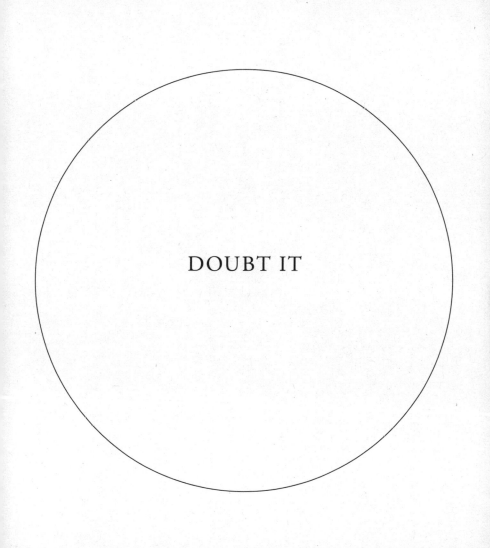

DOUBT IT

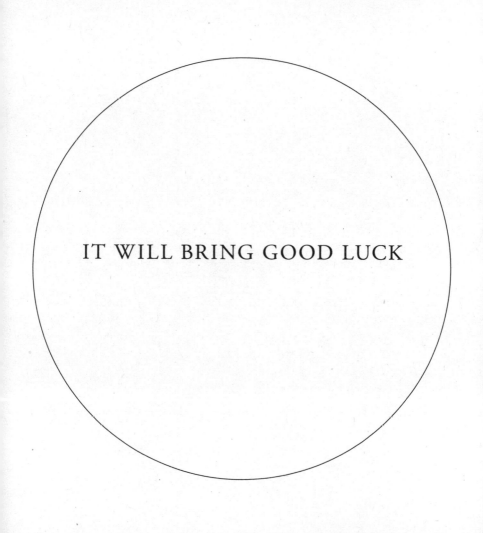

IT WILL BRING GOOD LUCK

IT MAY BE CHALLENGING, BUT
YOU WILL FIND VALUE IN IT

BE PATIENT

YOU WILL FIND OUT EVERYTHING
YOU'LL NEED TO KNOW

THERE IS A SUBSTANTIAL LINK
TO ANOTHER SITUATION

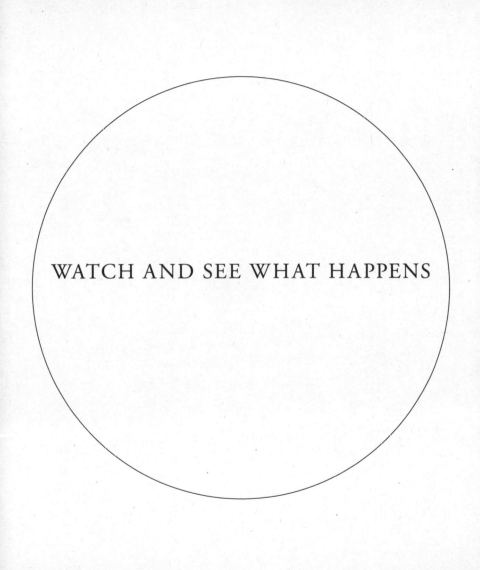

WATCH AND SEE WHAT HAPPENS

YOU KNOW BETTER NOW THAN
EVER BEFORE

IT WILL AFFECT HOW OTHERS
SEE YOU

RECONSIDER YOUR APPROACH

YOU'LL BE HAPPY YOU DID

GET IT IN WRITING

UNFAVORABLE AT THIS TIME

IT IS NOT SOMETHING TO BE
TAKEN LIGHTLY

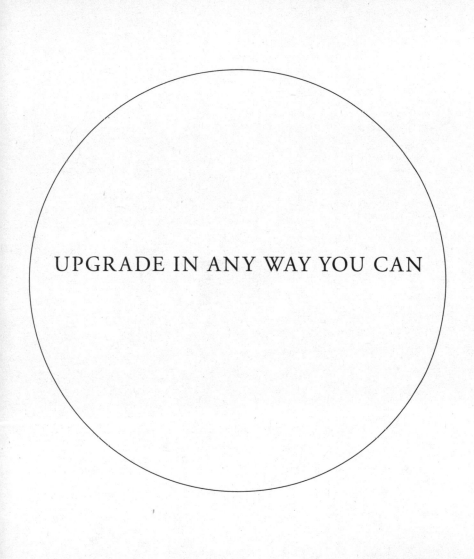

UPGRADE IN ANY WAY YOU CAN

IF YOU DO AS YOU'RE TOLD

IF IT'S DONE WELL; IF NOT,
DON'T DO IT AT ALL

DON'T ASK FOR ANY MORE
AT THIS TIME

AVOID THE FIRST SOLUTION

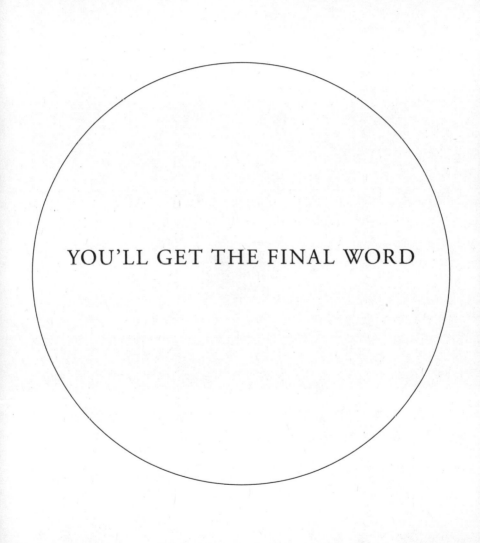

YOU'LL GET THE FINAL WORD

PROCEED AT A MORE
RELAXED PACE

THE BEST SOLUTION MAY NOT BE
THE OBVIOUS ONE

REMAIN FLEXIBLE

RESPECT THE RULES

TAKE THE LEAD

CHOOSE YOUR WORDS
THOUGHTFULLY

YOU MAY BE HANGING ON TO AN
OUTDATED IDEAL

THERE MAY BE A STRUGGLE

YOU'LL HAVE THE ENTHUSIASM
YOU'LL NEED

PROVIDED YOU SAY "THANK YOU"

ENJOY THE EXPERIENCE

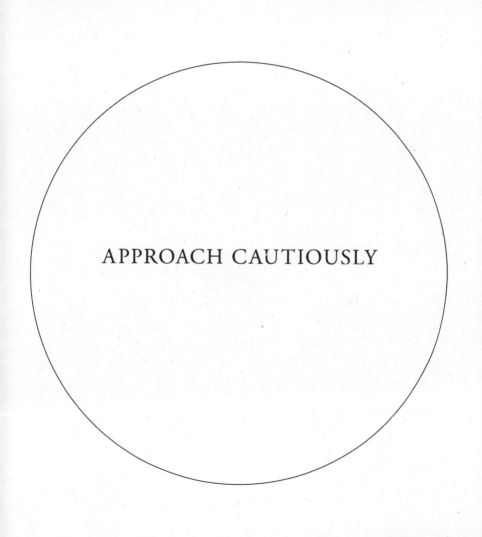

APPROACH CAUTIOUSLY

BE YOUR OWN BEST ADVOCATE

BE HAPPY FOR ANOTHER

PAY ATTENTION TO THE DETAILS

WATCH YOUR STEP AS YOU GO

SPEAK UP ABOUT IT

DON'T HESITATE

THIS IS A GOOD TIME TO MAKE A
NEW PLAN

MOVE ON

A STRONG COMMITMENT WILL
ACHIEVE GOOD RESULTS

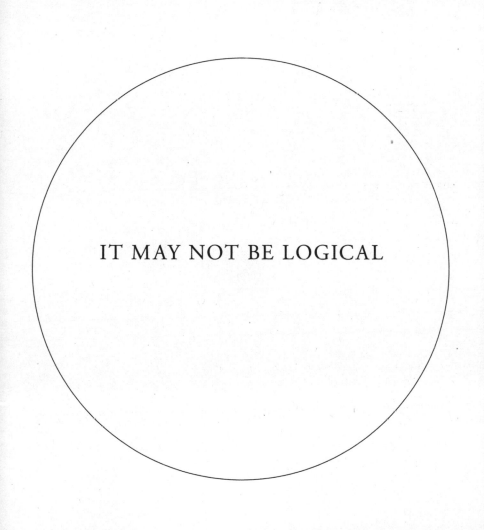

IT MAY NOT BE LOGICAL

THERE IS NO GUARANTEE

THE CIRCUMSTANCES COULD
CHANGE VERY QUICKLY

DON'T GET CAUGHT UP
IN YOUR EMOTIONS

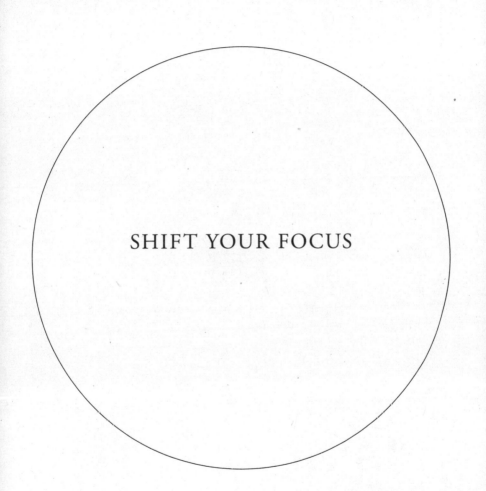

SHIFT YOUR FOCUS

08/05/2020

IT IS SIGNIFICANT

REPRIORITIZE
WHAT IS IMPORTANT

MAKE A LIST OF WHY NOT

DON'T WAIT

TAKE YOUR TIME

THERE IS GOOD REASON
TO BE OPTIMISTIC

IT IS SOMETHING YOU WON'T
FORGET

SEEK OUT MORE OPTIONS

FOLLOW THROUGH ON YOUR
OBLIGATIONS

DEAL WITH IT LATER

REVEAL YOUR THOUGHTS TO A
TRUSTED CONFIDANTE

FOLLOW SOMEONE ELSE'S LEAD

YOU COULD FIND YOURSELF
UNABLE TO COMPROMISE

MAKE A LIST OF WHY

TAKE A CHANCE

YOUR ACTIONS WILL
IMPROVE THINGS

ASK FOR HELP

KNOW WHEN IT'S TIME TO GO

ACCEPT A CHANGE TO YOUR
ROUTINE

YOU'LL NEED TO TAKE THE INITIATIVE

YOU'LL HAVE TO COMPROMISE

YOU NEED MORE INFORMATION

TRUST YOUR ORIGINAL THOUGHT

SEEK OUT THE PATH OF LEAST
RESISTANCE

IT WILL CREATE A STIR

YOU'LL OVERCOME
ANY OBSTACLES

IT WOULD BE BETTER TO FOCUS
ON YOUR WORK

IT WILL BE A PLEASURE

BE MORE GENEROUS

BET ON IT

GOOD THINGS ARE SEEKING

YOU OUT

DON'T LEAVE ROOM FOR REGRET

MAKE A CONTRIBUTION

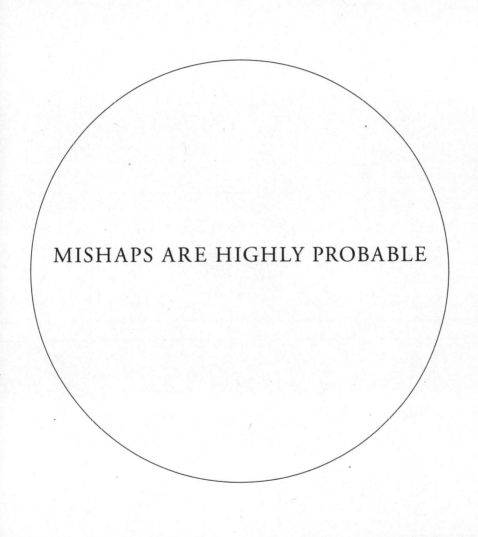

MISHAPS ARE HIGHLY PROBABLE

PRESS FOR CLOSURE

REALIZE THAT TOO MANY
CHOICES CAN BE AS DIFFICULT
AS TOO FEW

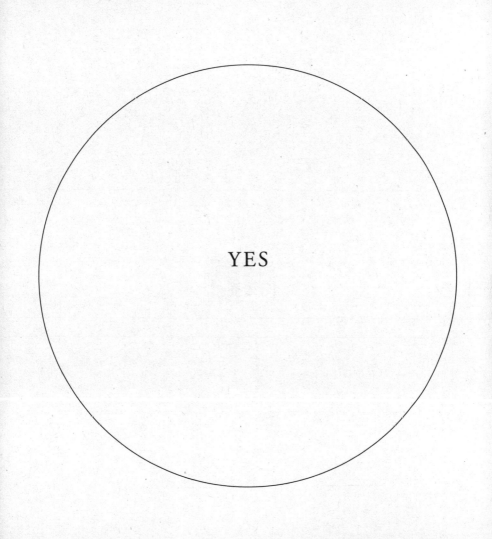

LISTEN CAREFULLY; THEN
YOU WILL KNOW

THE ANSWER
IS IN YOUR BACKYARD

LAUGH ABOUT IT

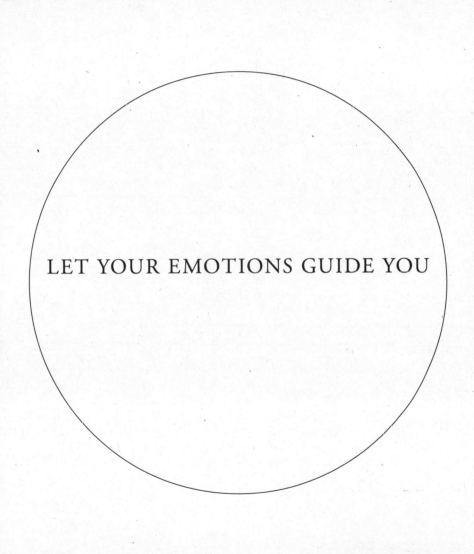

LET YOUR EMOTIONS GUIDE YOU

OTHERS WILL DEPEND ON YOUR
CHOICES

LET IT GO

IT'S TIME FOR YOU TO GO

DON'T BE DISTRACTED

GIVE IT ALL YOU'VE GOT

YOU DON'T REALLY CARE

YOU'LL NEED TO CONSIDER
OTHER WAYS

A YEAR FROM NOW
IT WON'T MATTER

FOLLOW THE ADVICE OF EXPERTS

IT COULD BE EXTRAORDINARY

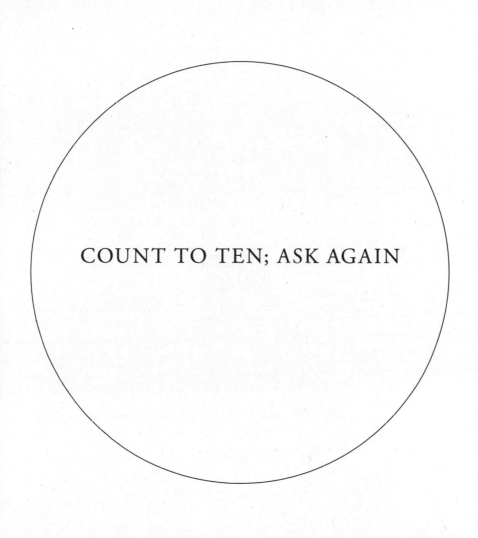

COUNT TO TEN; ASK AGAIN

ACT AS THOUGH IT IS
ALREADY REAL

SETTING PRIORITIES WILL BE A
NECESSARY PART OF THE PROCESS

USE YOUR IMAGINATION

IT'S GONNA BE GREAT

TO ENSURE THE BEST
DECISION, BE CALM

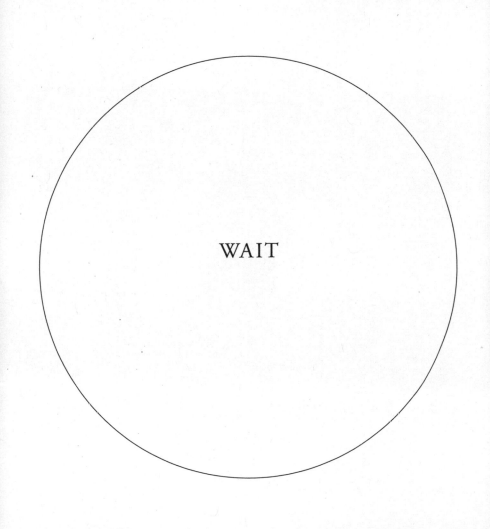

WAIT

YOU'LL HAVE TO MAKE IT UP
AS YOU GO

FOLLOW THE DIRECTIONS

UNQUESTIONABLY

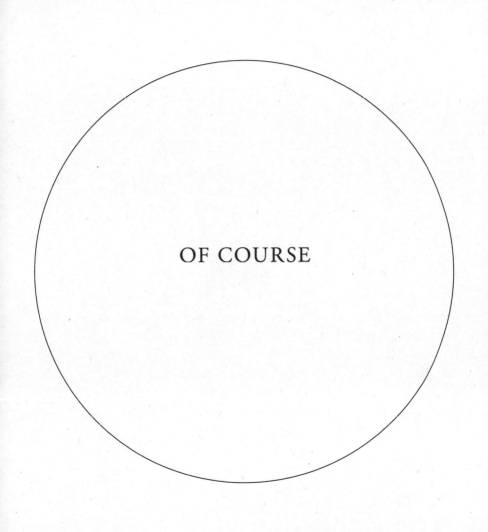

OF COURSE

LOOK FOR WHAT MAY BE HIDDEN

YOU KNOW BETTER NOW THAN
EVER BEFORE

TRUST YOUR INTUITION

DON'T MISS AN OPPORTUNITY

ASK YOUR FATHER

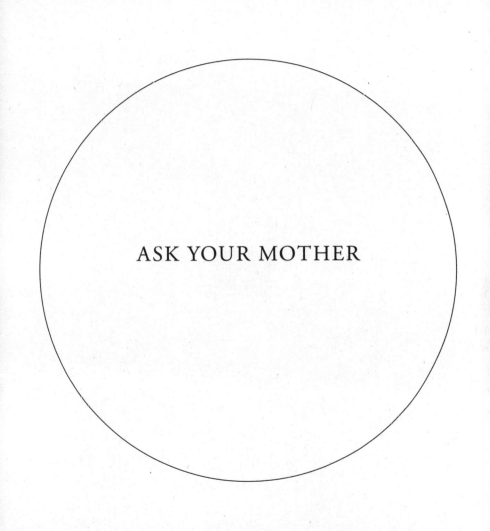

ASK YOUR MOTHER

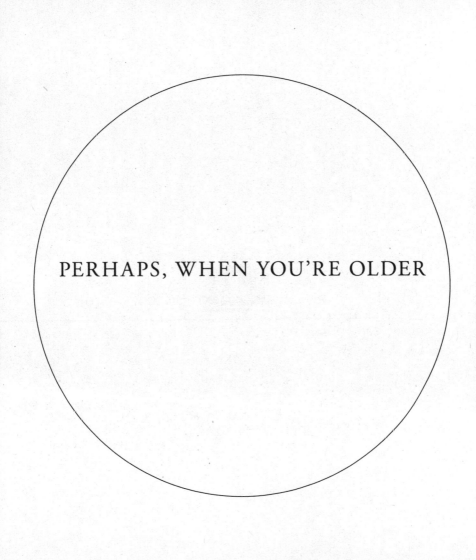

PERHAPS, WHEN YOU'RE OLDER

FINISH SOMETHING ELSE FIRST

YOU MAY HAVE OPPOSITION

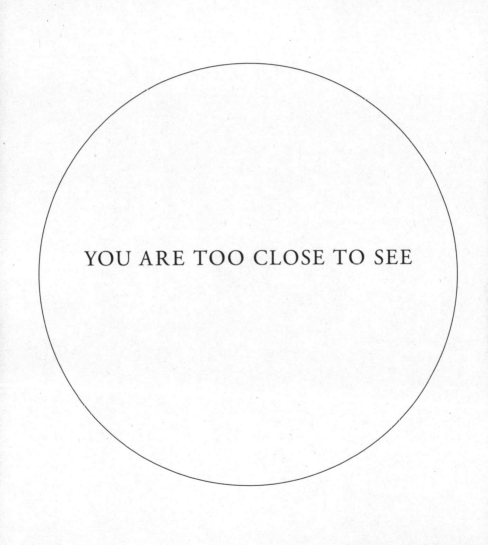

YOU ARE TOO CLOSE TO SEE

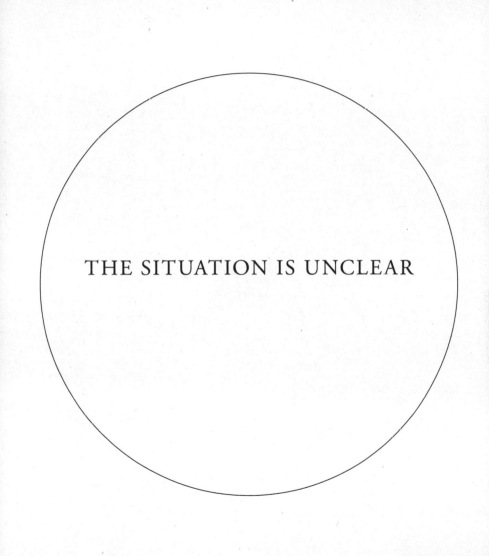

THE SITUATION IS UNCLEAR

A SUBSTANTIAL EFFORT

WILL BE REQUIRED

ALLOW YOURSELF TO REST FIRST

THE CHANCE WILL NOT
COME AGAIN SOON

THE ANSWER MAY COME TO YOU
IN ANOTHER LANGUAGE

RECONSIDER YOUR APPROACH

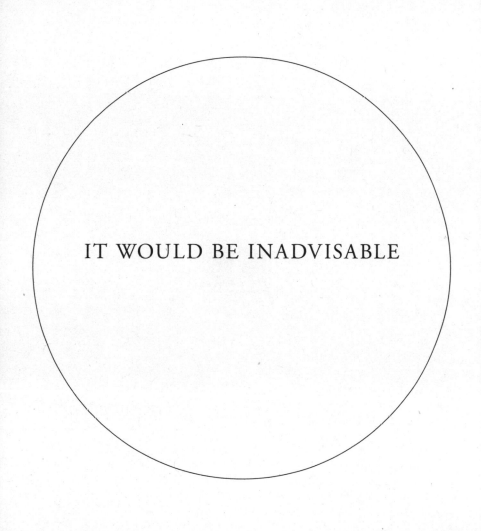

IT WOULD BE INADVISABLE

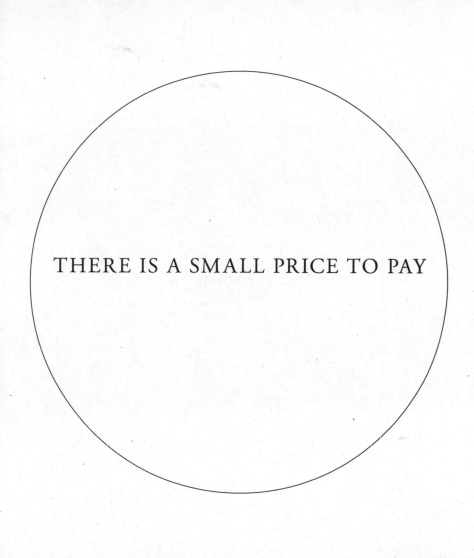

THERE IS A SMALL PRICE TO PAY

WAIT FOR A BETTER OFFER

SETTLE IT SOON

REMAIN OBJECTIVE

YES, BUT DON'T FORCE IT

GET A CLEARER VIEW

BE DELIGHTFULLY SURE OF IT

NOW YOU CAN

PROVIDED YOU SAY "THANK YOU"

DON'T OVERDO IT

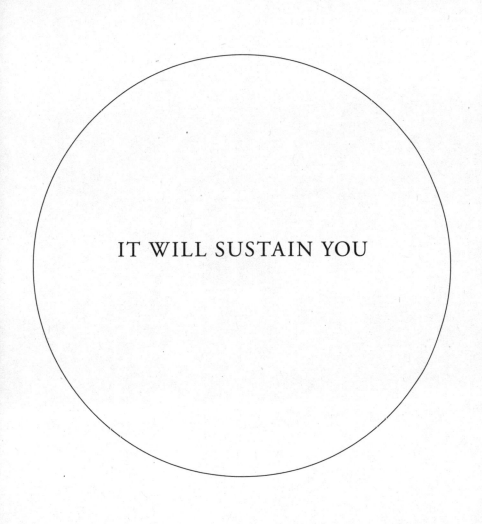

IT WILL SUSTAIN YOU

IT COULD COST YOU

ADOPT AN ADVENTUROUS
ATTITUDE

IT IS SURE TO MAKE THINGS
INTERESTING

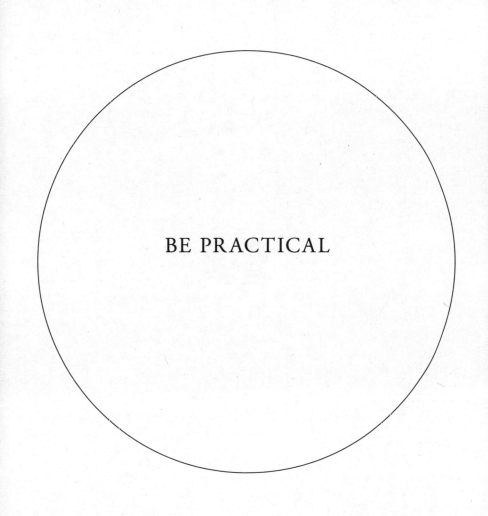

BE PRACTICAL

ARE YOU READY?

SAVE YOUR ENERGY

PAY ATTENTION TO THE DETAILS

IT IS CERTAIN

IT IS UNCERTAIN

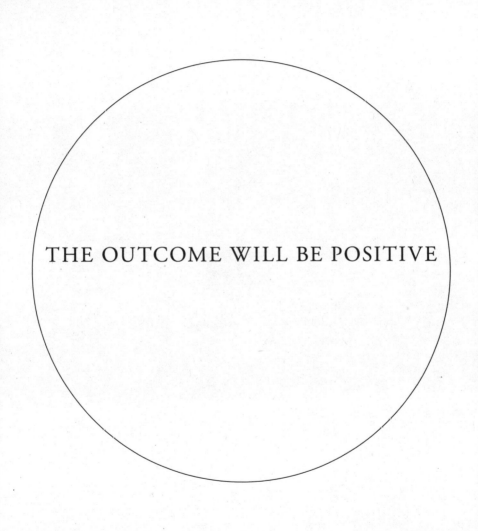

THE OUTCOME WILL BE POSITIVE

YOU MAY HAVE TO DROP
OTHER THINGS

DON'T BE CONCERNED

PREPARE FOR THE UNEXPECTED

TELL SOMEONE WHAT IT MEANS
TO YOU

WHATEVER YOU DO, THE RESULTS
WILL BE LASTING

KEEP AN OPEN MIND

IT'S A GOOD TIME TO MAKE PLANS

IT MAY BE AMBITIOUS, BUT YOU
WILL FIND VALUE IN IT

IT IS WORTH THE TROUBLE

YOU'LL OVERCOME
ANY OBSTACLES

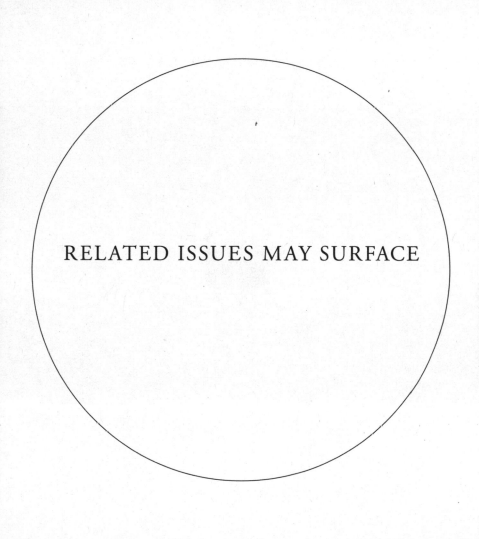

RELATED ISSUES MAY SURFACE

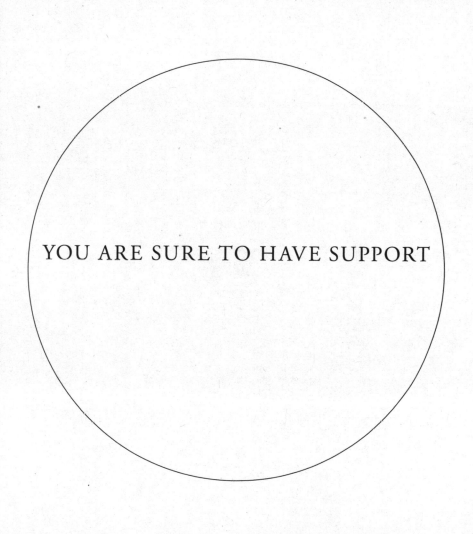

YOU ARE SURE TO HAVE SUPPORT

ASSISTANCE WOULD MAKE YOUR
PROGRESS A SUCCESS

COLLABORATION WILL BE
THE KEY

SEEK OUT MORE OPTIONS

TAKE CHARGE

IT CANNOT FAIL

YOU MUST ACT NOW

RESPECT THE RULES

GENTLE PERSISTENCE WILL

PAY OFF

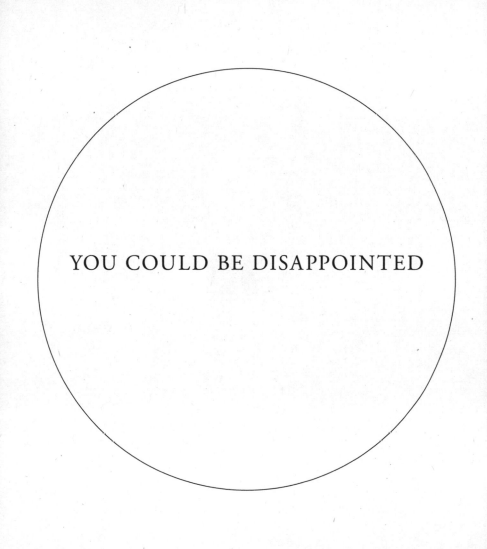

YOU COULD BE DISAPPOINTED

IT MAY ALREADY BE A DONE DEAL

FOLLOW THROUGH WITH YOUR
GOOD INTENTIONS

TAKE MORE TIME TO DECIDE

FOLLOW THROUGH ON YOUR
OBLIGATIONS

DON'T BE PRESSURED INTO
ACTING TOO QUICKLY

DON'T IGNORE THE OBVIOUS

OTHERS WILL RESPECT

YOUR CHOICES

DON'T BE TOO PRACTICAL

BE A GOOD ROLE MODEL

IT'S NOT WORTH A STRUGGLE

LISTEN CAREFULLY; THEN
YOU WILL KNOW

DON'T FORGET TO HAVE FUN

DON'T DOUBT IT

A STRONG COMMITMENT WILL
ACHIEVE GOOD RESULTS

TRY A MORE UNLIKELY SOLUTION

LEAVE BEHIND OLD SOLUTIONS

KEEP IT TO YOURSELF

WATCH YOUR STEP AS YOU GO

EXPLORE IT WITH PLAYFUL
CURIOSITY

DON'T BE TOO DEMANDING

DON'T LEAVE ROOM FOR REGRET

ACT AS THOUGH IT IS
ALREADY REAL

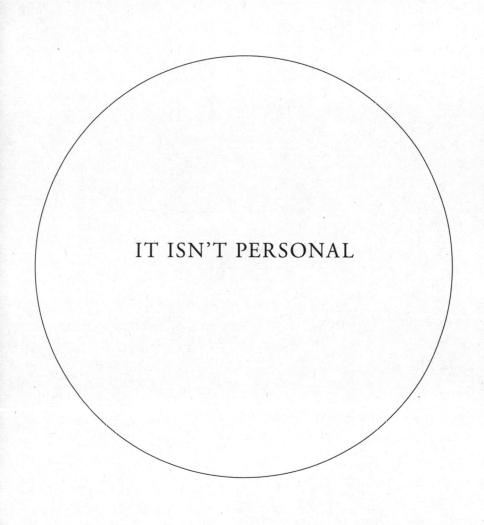

IT ISN'T PERSONAL

BE PERSISTENT

CHOOSE WHAT WILL MAKE

YOU HAPPY

DON'T LET MONEY DECIDE IT

IT WILL WORK ITSELF OUT

IF IT'S TOO DIFFICULT,
MAYBE IT'S NOT YOURS

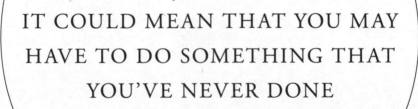

IT COULD MEAN THAT YOU MAY
HAVE TO DO SOMETHING THAT
YOU'VE NEVER DONE

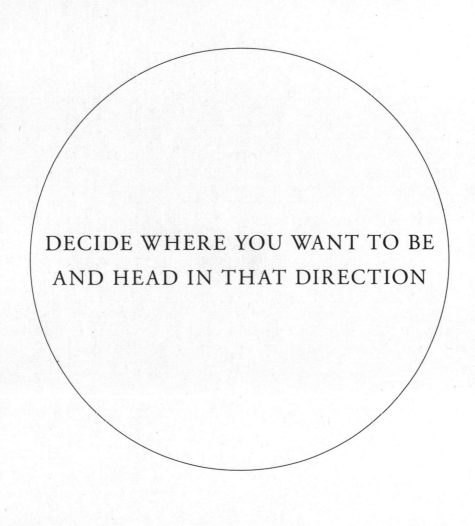

DECIDE WHERE YOU WANT TO BE
AND HEAD IN THAT DIRECTION

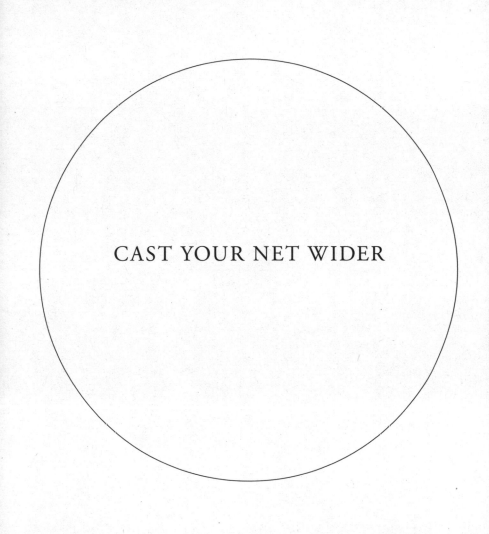

CAST YOUR NET WIDER

MAKE NO ASSUMPTIONS

RESPECT THE FUNDAMENTALS

BE RESOURCEFUL

FIND MORE TIME

NOTHING WILL COMPARE

IT WILL BE AN OPPORTUNITY

DON'T GIVE UP YOUR RIGHT
TO WAIT

BE DELIBERATE

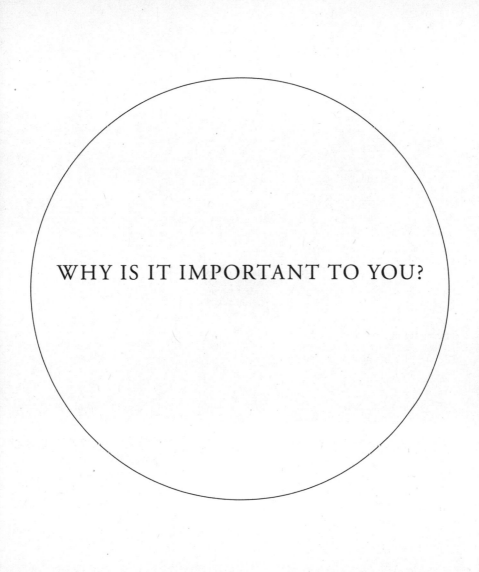

WHY IS IT IMPORTANT TO YOU?

DON'T LET THE MOMENT PASS

YOU'LL GET WHAT YOU
SETTLE FOR

CHOOSE WHATEVER WILL
HELP YOU TO GROW

BE KIND

REALIZE THAT TOO MANY
CHOICES CAN BE AS DIFFICULT
AS TOO FEW

TAKE A CHANCE

YOU WILL HAVE EVERYTHING
NECESSARY FOR YOUR SUCCESS

OTHERS MAY NOT APPROVE

YOU'LL HAVE THE STRENGTH
YOU'LL NEED

INITIATE AN ADVENTURE

BE TACTFUL

YOU'LL NEED TO CONSIDER
OTHER WAYS

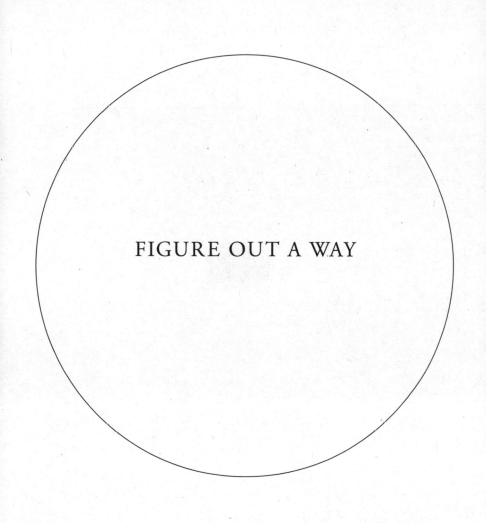

FIGURE OUT A WAY

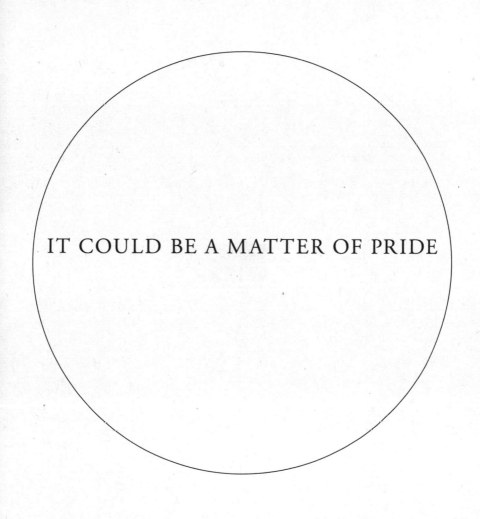

IT COULD BE A MATTER OF PRIDE

PURSUE MORE VARIETY

DON'T GET CAUGHT UP
IN YOUR EMOTIONS

PITCH IN WHATEVER YOU CAN

ARRIVE EARLY

NO MATTER WHAT

YOU ARE TOO CLOSE TO SEE

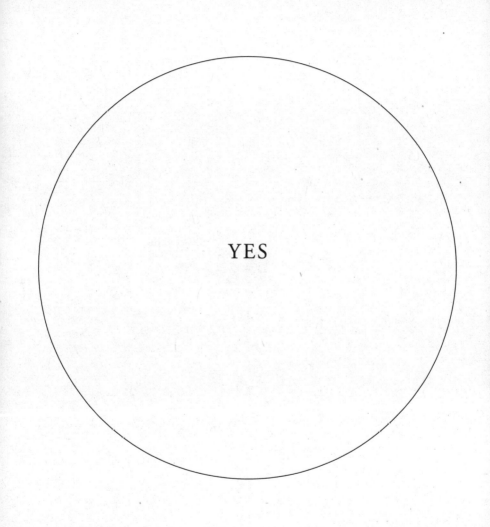

DON'T TAKE A CHANCE

IT IS NOT SOMETHING TO BE
TAKEN LIGHTLY

BE CONTENT TO LEAVE WELL
ENOUGH ALONE

TOO MUCH ATTENTION IS
ON THE DETAILS

KEEP IT LIGHT

GET MORE SLEEP

RECONSIDER ANOTHER
POSSIBILITY

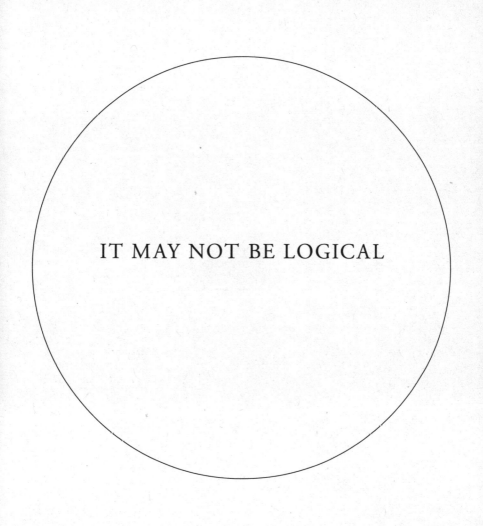

IT MAY NOT BE LOGICAL

THE ANSWER IS IN YOUR
BACKYARD

MAKE A CONTRIBUTION

USE YOUR IMAGINATION

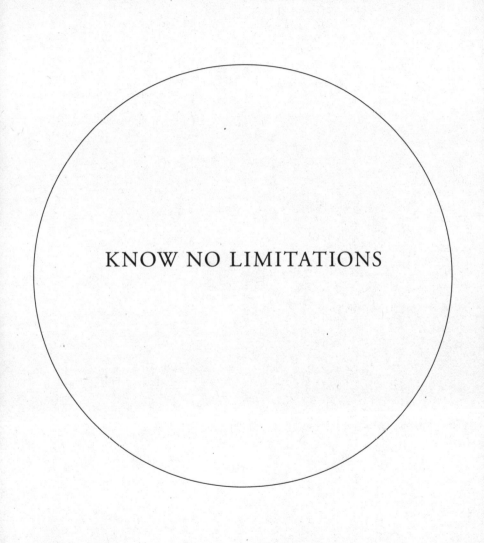

KNOW NO LIMITATIONS

BUILD SOMETHING BIGGER

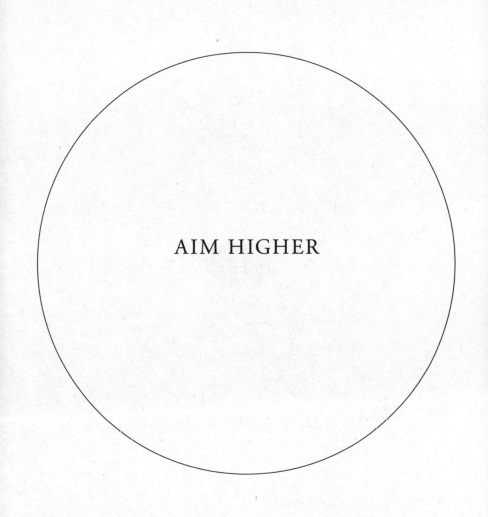

AIM HIGHER

TAKE IT IN STRIDE

BE A GOOD SPORT

TAKE THE LEAD

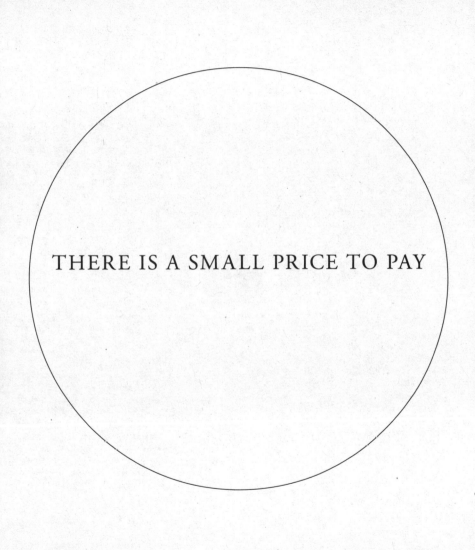

THERE IS A SMALL PRICE TO PAY

DON'T BE TOO CRITICAL

PUT YOUR FEELINGS IN
THE RIGHT PLACE

IDENTIFY WHAT MATTERS
ABOUT IT

HOW THINGS TURN OUT
WILL DEPEND ON YOU

LOOK FOR WHAT MAY BE HIDDEN

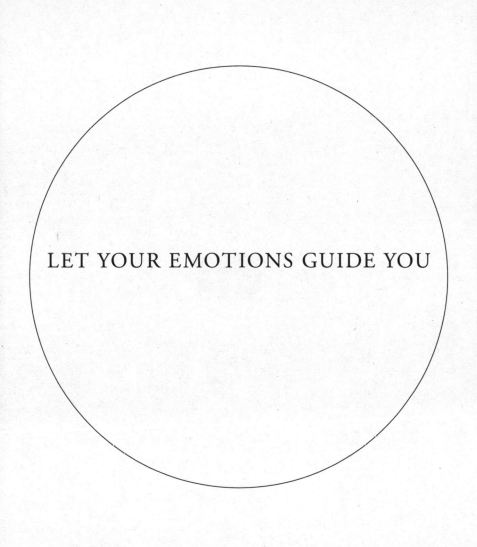

LET YOUR EMOTIONS GUIDE YOU

REVEAL YOUR THOUGHTS TO A
TRUSTED CONFIDANTE

TAKE A CLOSER LOOK

DON'T BE CONCERNED

YOU CAN DO THIS ON YOUR OWN

ASK FOR HELP

CREATE MORE SPACE FOR IT

DIVERT YOUR ATTENTION

WHAT DO YOU WANT?

DO YOUR BEST TO SET THE
STANDARD

THERE IS GOOD REASON
TO BE OPTIMISTIC

DON'T BE DISTRACTED

ENJOY A NEW SETTING

YOU WILL NEED TO
ACCOMMODATE

REMAIN OBJECTIVE

TELL SOMEONE WHAT IT MEANS
TO YOU

CONSIDER IT AN OPPORTUNITY

SEEK OUT THE PATH OF LEAST
RESISTANCE

GOOD THINGS ARE SEEKING

YOU OUT

IT WON'T MATTER WHEN YOU DO,
BUT THAT YOU DO

YOU MAY BE HANGING ON TO AN
OUTDATED IDEAL

IT'LL CHANGE YOUR LUCK

DON'T RESIST

FOLLOW THE DIRECTIONS

THE BEST SOLUTION MAY BE
THE OBVIOUS ONE

DON'T BE TOO CAUTIOUS

YOU MAY REGRET IT

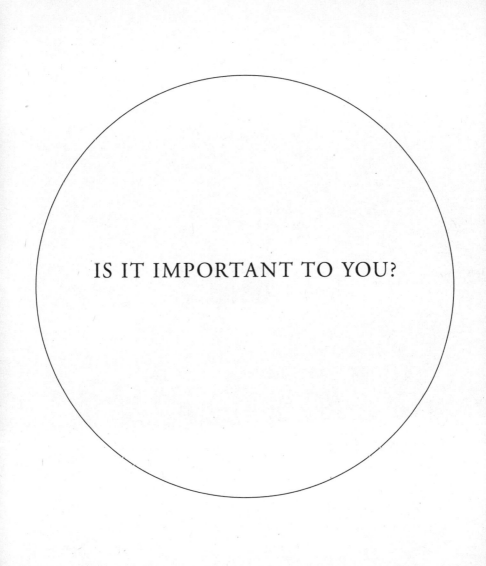

IS IT IMPORTANT TO YOU?

CHOOSE YOUR WORDS
CAREFULLY

LIMIT THE OPTIONS

FOCUS YOUR ATTENTION

SHOULDN'T YOU BE OUTSIDE
PLAYING?

WOULD IT BE A PLEASURE?

BE ON TIME

ASK YOUR FATHER

ASK YOUR MOTHER

TAKE YOUR TIME

YES, BUT DON'T FORCE IT

THERE IS MORE TO KNOW

FIND OUT THE FACTS

NOT IF YOU'RE ALONE

UNCOVER MORE DETAILS

YOUR HEART ISN'T IN IT

BE HAPPY FOR ANOTHER

YOU ARE FAVORED

NEVER

A YEAR FROM NOW
IT WON'T MATTER

ARE YOU READY?

YOU MUST

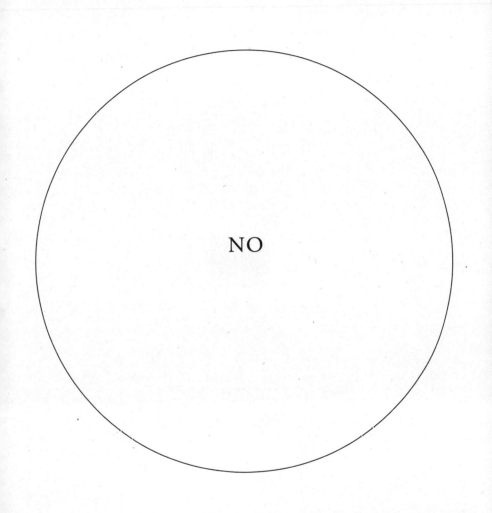

CONSERVE YOUR RESOURCES

BE A GOOD ROLE MODEL

NEGOTIATE A BETTER DEAL

FAVOR THE GOOD THINGS

DON'T LET IT BE RUINED BY
REASON

SLEEP ON IT

DO YOUR BEST

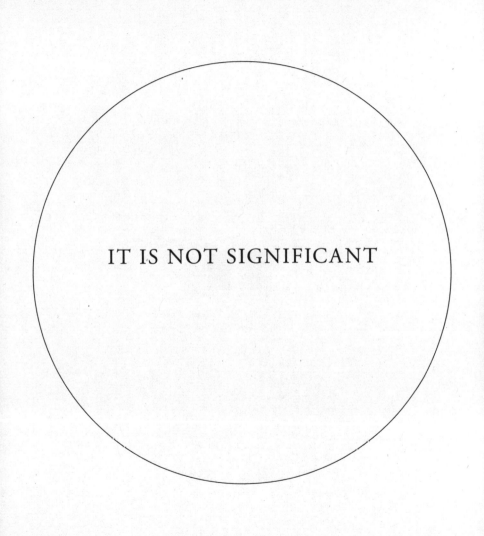

IT IS NOT SIGNIFICANT

YOU HAVE SO MUCH TO OFFER

KNOW WHAT'S IMPORTANT
TO YOU

YOU DESERVE THE BEST

BETTER THINGS ARE
SEEKING YOU OUT

IT'S UP TO YOU

CHOOSE WHAT MAKES
YOU HAPPY

LET YOUR HEART LEAD THE WAY

DON'T GET CAUGHT UP
IN THE DETAILS

ACKNOWLEDGMENTS

Thank you to my agents at Victoria Sanders Literary Agency: Victoria, Bernadette, Jessica, and Diane. You took a chance on my project twenty years ago and it's been a pleasure ever since. I offer my deepest thanks and appreciation to you.

Hachette Books: Thanks to Amanda, Mollie, Becky, and Mauro for designing a new edition, the opportunity to dig around in some of my favorite places—libraries and bookstores—and the willingness to include me on the team to repackage a project that is so dear to me. Cheers to celebrating twenty years of having all the answers!

Thank you to the Seattle Public Library; every Seattle branch is my new favorite over and over again. My library card remains one of my most prized possessions.